# A SHIFT IN PERSPECTIVE

# A SHIFT IN PERSPECTIVE

*Seeing Motherhood Differently*

**KAITLIN FOLSE LEBEOUF**

First published by Kaitlin Folse LeBeouf 2025

Copyright© 2025 by Kaitlin Folse LeBeouf

All rights reserved. No part of this publication may be reproduced, stored or transmitted in any form or by any means, electronic, mechanical, photocopying, recording, scanning, or otherwise without written permission from the publisher. It is illegal to copy this book, post it to a website, or distribute it by any other means without permission.

Scripture quotations are taken from the Holy Bible, New Living Translation (NLT), copyright© 1996, 2004, 2015 by Tyndale House Foundation. Used by permission. All rights reserved.

First edition

ISBN: 979-8-9940344-0-8

This book was professionally typeset on Reedsy.

Find out more at reedsy.com

For my girls, Livie and Emmie— the ones who made me into a mama. You challenge me, teach me, and draw me closer to Jesus every single day. This book belongs to you as much as it does to me.

# Contents

Introduction ............................................................... 9
The Overwhelmed Mama ........................................... 13
Snooze the Chaos, Please ........................................... 18
The Mom Win That... Wasn't ..................................... 23
Can I Just Take a Bath in Peace? ................................ 27
Was I Mean Today? .................................................... 33
Fall, Winter, Spring... and Motherhood .................... 39
Bypassing Dad –Straight to Mom ............................... 45
When the Mom Anxiety Gets Loud ........................... 52
Apparently... I'm the One With the Attitude ............ 58
No Secrets - Just Truth ............................................... 63
Press Your Heart ......................................................... 68
Shoes or No Shoes ...................................................... 73
Teaching Tiny Hearts ................................................. 78
Letter to The Mamas .................................................. 84
Letter to My Mama ..................................................... 88
Letter to My Girls ....................................................... 91
Daily Perspective Prayers ........................................... 94
Closing ........................................................................ 96

# Introduction

*I* kept finding myself telling my friends — and even my own mom — how I was feeling lately. I kept asking, "Do you ever feel like a bad mom? Because I swear I feel like the worst sometimes." I felt short-tempered, impatient, and like I was blowing up over the smallest things. I didn't want to play every night. I didn't feel fun. I didn't feel soft.

But the truth is:
It's okay to feel overwhelmed.
It's okay to feel guilty.
It's okay to question yourself.

Not because you're a bad mama — but because you are a **good** one. Good mamas care deeply, love fiercely, and stress because we pour so much of ourselves into our kids — sometimes too much. We try to fill everyone else's cup from an empty one.

Then there's the nonstop mental load:
"It's Monday — did I send a new blanket for my Pre-K kiddo?"
"Did I pack lunches? Because who eats school lunch anymore, right?"
"Dance tonight for this kid."
"Homework due Thursday."
"Oh wait… soccer practice got moved again."

Who knew 4- and 6-year-old kids could have full weekly schedules? Three nights of dance, soccer practices for both, school events, work, dinner, laundry — I'm constantly coming and going. I'm not a bad mama. I'm a dang good mama who loves her kids so much — I'm just a tired one.

But guilt? That creeps in fast.
"You're not doing enough," it whispers.
Even while your kids are fed, safe, loved, and wearing clean clothes — most of the time.
(Folded? Absolutely not. Unless my mom comes help with the mountain on my sofa.) I want my kids to have everything — to feel loved, supported, involved, confident. And sometimes that desire, that love, is exactly what drains me. It's why I'm running on empty — why I'm crazy or a "couyon" most days (for my non down-the-bayou people — meaning crazy).

And this…
this is where **faith** entered my motherhood
in a real way.

I grew up in a home where we went to church, and I always knew about Jesus. But it wasn't until I hit a point where I genuinely couldn't handle the everyday mental load anymore — the schedules, the guilt, the overwhelm, the worry — that I finally said, "Okay Jesus… I need clarity. I need peace. I need **You**." And that's when I really started to feel Him.

I'm not a know-it-all Christian.
I don't have the Bible memorized.
I'm not in a season where I can sit for hours reading the Bible— I read when I can.

And that's okay. I'm raising kids. I'm managing life. And Jesus isn't asking for perfection — just presence.

**"Jesus, show me I'm not showing up alone."**

That prayer changed everything for me. And as I started writing this book, I realized I was answering the question I kept asking: "Am I a bad mom?" No. You're a good mama — that's why you're questioning. Good mamas self-check, care too much, and feel deeply.

As I wrote, I started to see the good in myself again.
The beauty inside the chaos.
The tenderness inside the frustration.
The strength inside the overwhelm.

It's all perspective — and sometimes all we need is a *shift*. Honestly, I think God let me walk through all this chaos recently with the purpose of this book— so I could put real, honest, raw truth in these pages for the mamas who need it. There will be good days, bad days, trying days. Days we lose it. Days we win big. Days we feel like champions. Days we cry in the bathroom.

But through all of it?
I'm giving it to **Jesus**.

My guilt.
My anxiety.

My overwhelm.
My kids.
My love.
My perspective.

Here's some real-life testimonies — straight from one tired, loving, overwhelmed mama to another. Here's to *shifting your perspective*. Here's to remembering you're doing better than you think. Here's to grace — for you and for them.

# The Overwhelmed Mama

Some days the chaos feels like it hits before I even fully wake up. There are days I dread picking up my kids from school — not because I don't love them, but because I already know what's coming. The sass. The attitude. The meltdowns before dinner. The arguments over the iPad. The constant needs when my tank is already empty. I love my babies with my whole heart… but sometimes I pray for bedtime like it's salvation.
And then the guilt hits me just as fast — the disappointment in myself that I'm looking forward to the quiet more than the moment.

And yet…

During those quiet moments at night, when the house finally settles and everyone is sleeping? That's when my mind starts wandering. That's when the guilt creeps in.

When the
"I should've been more patient"
and
"I should've done better"
thoughts attack the hardest.

But God... I'm blessed beyond measure. I begged for these kids. I walked through years of infertility, heartbreak, miscarriages, an ectopic pregnancy, surgery, and a lost tube just to get to them. And here I am — frustrated, overwhelmed, exhausted.

And then I remember...

Even if a child was a surprise blessing,
or conceived easily,
or came after years of waiting —

it **is** still normal for a mama to feel tired, stretched thin, and emotionally wrung out.

We carry so much.
We are the nurturers by design.
We feel deeply.
We love fiercely.
We break a little when they break.

I'll tell their dad, "Babe, correct her please." But the minute he does, I'm like, "Excuse you... be nice to her. That's my baby." It's the mother heart — soft and protective, even when they make us absolutely insane. And I mean it — **INSANE**.

At night, I lay with them until they fall asleep. We argue about the iPad —

"Just five more minutes!"
"No, I'm not picking it back up."

And yes… I'm arguing with a 4-year-old.

Because she's strong-willed. Because I raised her that way — and it'll be a blessing one day. She'll probably be president… or running something illegal. (Honestly, it could go either way.)

The other night I told her, "Emmie, you need to pray for your attitude and patience." She huffed. She puffed. She fussed. But then she said,

"Mom, let's pray."

So we did.

And in the middle of her tiny chaos and big feelings, she whispered:

"Dear heavenly God…
please let us have a good day at school,
and patience for myself,
and let our hearts keep beeping."

And suddenly, in another perspective…

**Maybe I'm not doing so bad after all.**

## PRAYER

Jesus,
Meet me in the chaos.
Meet me in the moments where motherhood feels like too much.

Remind me that frustration doesn't mean failure.
Remind me that exhaustion doesn't mean I don't love my kids.

Give me grace for the hard moments,
and peace in the quiet ones.

Help me see the beauty You're weaving
through our imperfect days.

And thank You for these babies —
the ones I begged You for,
the ones I love more than anything,
the ones who teach me patience, love,
and how deeply I need You.

**Amen.**

## REFLECTION QUESTIONS

*Take a moment to pause, breathe, and think about your day. Let these questions help you realize what mattered, what challenged you, and what blessed you.*

1. What's one moment from today that I could view through a different perspective?

2. When did I feel most overwhelmed today, and how could I remind myself that feeling overwhelmed doesn't mean I'm failing?

3. What part of this chapter made me feel seen or understood as a mama?

# Snooze the Chaos, Please

Some mornings make me want to hit the snooze button on motherhood itself. Before the sun is up, before my favorite soda even thinks about kicking in, the chaos has already begun. School mornings are their own special brand of madness. I pray for peacefulness, for minimal meltdowns, for just one morning where everything goes smoothly. But somehow, whether we wake up two hours early or thirty-five minutes before the school bell, the outcome always feels the same: we are turning into that school parking lot on two wheels, praying we don't get another truancy letter. (Not kidding… well, kind of kidding… but also not.)

It starts simple—"Fix my hair first!" Then immediately followed by, "No! I want THAT bow!" And then the lunchbox drama begins. The same lunchbox they found in the playroom that's been missing for two years is suddenly the only lunchbox on planet earth worth using. My kids will straight-up have emotional breakdowns over who gets the one they discovered at the bottom of a toy bin.

And here I am, with a job that allows me the blessing of getting my kids ready for school—and yet I still feel overwhelmed, rushed, chaotic, and guilty for wishing mornings were easier.

But here's the truth I'm learning:

Being overwhelmed doesn't mean I'm ungrateful.
Feeling flustered doesn't mean I'm failing.

It means I care.
It means I'm showing up.
It means I'm trying to pour from a cup that's running low—because I love them too much to stop trying.

Even on the mornings I'm drained, we say a little prayer on the four-minute-thirty-second drive to school. And today? Today my kids decided to fight about who got to pray first. One cut the other off. The one who said she didn't even want to go first slammed the car door because she didn't get to interrupt.

Yes. My kids can argue about who gets to pray first. Only in my house.

And in the moment, I wanted to scream.

But then… I felt a **shift**.

That little tug from God—
the reminder to change my perspective.

Because if my kids are fighting over who gets to pray...

maybe that's not chaos. Maybe that's a blessing I was too stressed to see.

So I've been trying different things. Waking them up gently. Playing music. Dancing around the room like a fool just to set a softer tone. Some days it works. Some days it flops HARD.

But I'm going to keep trying.

Because motherhood is just a series of attempts—
and God fills in the gaps we can't.

## PRAYER

Jesus,
Meet me in the morning chaos.
Help me breathe when everything feels
rushed, loud, or overwhelming.

Give me patience when the battles start
before breakfast.

Give me grace when I feel guilty
for wishing it was easier.

Remind me that even in the madness,
there are blessings tucked inside —
a strong-willed child, a silly argument,
a whispered prayer.

Help me see the good.
Help me shift my perspective.

And thank You for loving me even
in the moments when I'm barely
holding it together.

**Amen.**

## REFLECTION QUESTIONS

*Take a moment to pause, breathe, and think about your day. Let these questions help you realize what mattered, what challenged you, and what blessed you.*

1. What's one moment from today that I could view through a different perspective?

2. Where in my day could I have "snoozed the chaos" by pausing, breathing, or choosing calm?

3. Did a part of this chapter make me feel seen?

# The Mom Win That... Wasn't

S ome days, all I want is one mom **win**. Just one moment where I feel like, "Okay, yeah… I did that. That was good." But lately? I've felt like all I do is referee.

"Stop touching her."
"Give it back."
"Why are y'all fighting again?"
"Lord, I will lose my religion right here in this living room."

Then break up a fight. Stop a Meltdown. Try to prevent the next one—fail. Fuss. Apologize. Fuss again. Repeat.

So the other day, I picked the girls up from school—my husband was working late—and I thought, *Let me do something fun. Let me create a mom win*. "Girls," I said, "Let's go buy a new Christmas tree!" Because who has time to put lights on the old one that just decided to burn out? Not me. Not this season.

So off to town we went. And immediately… CHAOS. Meltdowns over who sits where in the cart (or buggey, for my down-the-bayou people). "Can I get a lollipop?" "Can I get this?" "Mom, look at this!" "Mom, I need that!" I blinked and thought, *Okay, I am so ready to just go home.*

We grabbed food on the way home—which took forever—and in that long drive-thru line, my phone rang with a work call I had to answer. Meanwhile, my kids were in the backseat absolutely dragging it out with each other over who even knows what at that point.

By the time we pulled into the driveway, I was overstimulated, overwhelmed, and genuinely considering going to bed at 6:15 p.m. And you know what? I didn't even put up the tree. The "mom win" I planned didn't happen. The magical moment I imagined? Didn't exist. I tried so hard… and it still went sideways.

And honestly? Looking back—**that's okay**.

Here's the truth I'm learning and another perspective: I'm human. I'm a mama who tries constantly for her kids. I show up, even when I'm tired, even when I'm fussing, even when I feel like I'm failing. I will always keep showing up. Some days I win. Some days I lose it. But I'll wake up tomorrow and **try again**—because that's what mamas do.

And maybe **that is the win**.

## PRAYER

Jesus,
Thank You for seeing my heart even on the days when nothing goes as planned.
When my "mom win" falls apart, remind me that my effort still matters.

Give me patience when chaos rises,
comfort when I feel overstimulated,
and grace when I lose my cool.

Help me remember that motherhood isn't about perfection —
it's about showing up, trying again, and loving deeply.

Thank You for tomorrow,
and thank You for the strength to try again.

**Amen.**

## **REFLECTION QUESTIONS**

*Take a moment to pause, breathe, and think about your day. Let these questions help you realize what mattered, what challenged you, and what blessed you.*

1. What's one moment from today that I could view through a different perspective?

2. Where did I show up today—even if it didn't go the way I hoped—and why does that still matter?

# Can I Just Take a Bath in Peace?

"Mom, your water is too hot… can you cool it down?"

No, baby. If you can't take the heat, get out the— …oh wait. Wrong saying. Never mind.

It **never** fails. My kids can be in the living room minding their business, watching a movie, playing together, not needing a single thing from me.

But the minute — the literal minute — I sneak into the bathroom to take a bath?

Two seconds in.
Water not even two inches high.

Here they come.

"Hey... can I come in?"

UGHHHHHH.

Sometimes I'm like, "Come back in five minutes. Let me just sit for a second."
Sometimes I'll say, "Ten minutes. Please."
And sometimes I catch myself thinking, *They're only little once... come on.*

And that's when the demands start:

"It's too hot."
"Scoot over."
"I was sitting by you first!"
"I want that toy!"
"Mom watch this!"
momwatchthismomwatchthismomwatchthis

And suddenly the bath that was supposed to help me unwind turns into one more place where I feel overwhelmed... and overstimulated... and DONE.

So I do what moms do — I get out.
I let them have the tub.
I go clean the bathroom counters, tidy up, pick up clothes on the floor — anything to just
mentally breathe.

While I'm straightening up, I hear them playing.
The giggles.

The splashes.
The "Mom, look! I'm a mermaid!"

And then the random deep questions from my 6-year-old like,

"Mom... do I have to work when I get older?"

My advice?

"Marry a rich man, sista."

Kidding...
(but it is true...)

People say, "Little kids, little problems," and it's true... but those little problems feel huge when they're happening every five seconds.

And somehow, I already miss these moments — even while I'm overwhelmed in them.

Lately it's felt like overstimulated chaos nonstop.
Noise, demands, questions, fighting, touching, fussing...
and me trying to hold myself together long enough to make it to bedtime.

So I'm challenging myself — and you — with a **different** perspective:

Pray to see the present.
Pray for peace in the chaos.
Pray for patience when your nerves are shot.
Pray to notice the sweetness tucked inside the noise.

Motherhood is loud… but it's good.
And I don't want to miss it because I'm too overwhelmed to notice the moments I'll wish
I could rewind one day.

## PRAYER

Jesus,
Meet me in the moments I'm just trying to take a bath in peace.
When I feel touched-out, drained, or overstimulated, remind me that
I'm human—
not a bad mom.

Give me patience for the little hands that need me
and grace for the moments I need space

Help me see the sweetness in their giggles,
the innocence in their questions,
and the blessings tucked inside the chaos.

Teach me to find the peace even when the bathroom becomes a playground.
and remind me that You're with me - even here in these moments.

**Amen.**

## REFLECTION QUESTIONS

*Take a moment to pause, breathe, and think about your day. Let these questions help you realize what mattered, what challenged you, and what blessed you.*

1. What's one moment from today that I could view through a different perspective?

2. When did I feel overstimulated or "touched-out" today, and how could I invite a little more patience, breathing room, or grace into that moment?

# Was I Mean Today?

The other day, I looked at my 6-year-old and asked, "Was I **mean** today?"

She shrugged and said,
"Eh… kinda."

Oh.
Wow.
Awesome.
Love that for me.

So I asked, "Why?"

She said, "Well… Emmie was acting kinda crazy in church this morning, and you fussed her. You told her she needed to stop."

Me, in my head:
Well… that sounds warranted to me.

"Anything else?" I asked.

"Nope."

And that was it.

Meanwhile, I had spent the ENTIRE afternoon overthinking every tone, every correction, every moment I felt short or impatient. I was convinced I'd ruined the day. I was replaying moments and labeling myself "mean," "too much," "too harsh," "not patient enough."

But my daughter?
She didn't notice any of that.
Just the one moment that actually made sense.

It made me realize something big:

Sometimes the battles we fight are completely **internal**.

We think we were terrible.
We think we were too rough.
We think we failed.

But our kids… they're just living their life.
Half the time they've moved on before we've finish feeling guilty.

As mothers, we hold ourselves to impossible standards.
We magnify our mistakes.
We obsess over our tone.
We judge ourselves harshly for moments our kids barely remember.

But here's the truth and a different perspective:

It is literally our job to teach our children.
To guide them.
To correct them.
To nurture **AND** discipline them.

We can't let them walk all over us — they're learning how to act, how to speak, how to treat others, how to handle emotions.

And they're watching us constantly.

And we're not always going to get it right.

We will blow up.
We will have rough days.
We will correct sharply sometimes.

And that doesn't make us bad moms — it makes us human.

The funny thing?

All the moments I thought I was too harsh, too short, too annoyed… she never even noticed.

Sometimes, we're fighting battles in our minds that never even happened out loud.

They don't need us to be perfect.
They need us to be present.
They need us to teach them.
They need us to model love and boundaries.

They need to see what humility looks like — including when we say sorry.

And honestly?
Saying sorry is hard.

Not just to our kids, but to our spouses, our friends, our family.

A simple, "Sorry babe," can feel like it weighs a hundred pounds.

But apologizing teaches our kids more than perfection ever could.

We're not their friend.
We're their mama.
Their example.
Their safe place.
Their teacher.

And we're doing **better** than we think.

## PRAYER

Jesus,
Help me quiet the battles I create in my own mind.
When I replay moments and judge myself harshly,
remind me that You see my heart first.

Give me grace to correct my children with love,
and wisdom to know when to apologize.
and grace when I lose my cool.

Help me see myself the way my kids see me —
not perfect, but present.
Not flawless, but faithful.

And when I worry that I've been too much or not enough,
remind me that You fill every gap I cannot.

**Amen.**

## REFLECTION QUESTIONS

*Take a moment to pause, breathe, and think about your day. Let these questions help you realize what mattered, what challenged you, and what blessed you.*

1. Did something happen today in my life that I could look at in a different way?

2. Is there a moment today I've been replaying in my head that my kids probably already moved past–or never even noticed?

2. Where can I give myself more grace today instead of guilt?

# Fall, Winter, Spring... and Motherhood

*I* love to read.
I always have.

Ever since my 5th-grade teacher read us The Chronicles of Narnia, something in me fell in love with stories.

Last year, I hit my reading goal of 40 books.
Forty.
I felt unstoppable.

This year?
Five.
With one month left.

But in the last four months, I've read and studied almost the entire book of John. So honestly… if I only read one thing this year, I'm glad it's that.

Maybe God knew what I needed more than another aesthetic, thick book stack.

And then there's this — I used to think as I was reading, "Can't be that hard to write a book." I'd try to just open my notes and start typing.

Yeah… no.
Wow.
Turns out it's harder than I thought.

But here I am — writing the book I never thought possible with words easily flowing from me.

And the wild thing?

God let me write it about the hardest and most rewarding season of my life:

Motherhood.

Because here's the truth I'm learning:

Life is made of seasons.
And the amount of "me time" you have depends on which one you're in.

I remember years ago, when I only had one child, I went to a friend's house. I opened the door and it smelled like straight-up fall Heaven. Pumpkin everything. It looked like a Pinterest board in there.

Meanwhile, my own fall decorations were still sitting in a dusty box in a closet. I hadn't even pulled them out yet.

And I felt jealous — like I missed the version of me who had time to decorate, who made everything smell like the holidays, who had seasonal pillows for every couch.

I came home that evening, walked into my kitchen, and opened the fridge. And right there… stuck to it with a magnet… was a potty-training chart.

A potty chart.
On my fridge.
With "Pee/Poop" written on it in big letters.

And I just laughed.

Like, HELLO, you prayed for these days.
And here they are.

This is the best decoration in the world.
Better than any candle or fall-scented diffuser I'll ever buy.

Another perspective unlocked.

Because that map-of-stickers and accidents and attempts?

It meant my baby was growing.
It meant these precious, chaotic days were happening right in front of me.

It doesn't matter that I didn't hit my reading goal — I read the most important book of all.

It doesn't matter that my house doesn't smell like "Pumpkin Maple Marshmallow Wonderland" or "Flannel Forest Cozy Cabin."

Because this season — this messy, loud, exhausting, beautiful season — is exactly what I prayed for.

Motherhood doesn't mean losing the old me.
It means she's evolving.
Growing.
Shifting.

Making room for a version of me that reads Scripture instead of not-so-Godly chapters, hangs potty charts instead of garlands, and finds joy in different places than before.

This is a new me — not a worse me.
Just a mama in a new season.

And I want to enjoy it while I'm in it.

## Prayer

Jesus,
Help me see the beauty in the season I'm in.
When I miss the old version of myself,
remind me that You are growing me into someone new.

Give me perspective when I compare,
peace when I feel behind,
and gratitude for the moments happening right in front of me.

Help me embrace this chapter of motherhood —
with all its noise, chaos, and love —
and show me how to enjoy the present
without longing for what was.

**Amen.**

## REFLECTION QUESTIONS

*Take a moment to pause, breathe, and think about your day. Let these questions help you realize what mattered, what challenged you, and what blessed you.*

1. Where in your current season can you see growth, even if it feels messy or slow?

2. How can you practice gratitude for the season you're in right now?

# Bypassing Dad – Straight to Mom

Sometimes I swear my husband is hiding in the bathroom until the kids move out.

Like… what is he even doing in there?
A full remodel?
Building a boat?
Launching a side business?

Meanwhile, all I want is to pee without someone busting through the door.

And it doesn't matter what I'm doing — these kids can sniff out MOM from anywhere.

I could be in the middle of performing heart surgery —
(God bless that imaginary patient) —
and my kids would STILL come running in like:

"Moooom… mooom… MOOOOMMM!"

"Sorry sir, let me go see what my child with zero patience needs."

"Yes baby? What is it?"

"Can I have a snack?"

"A snack? Isn't your dad literally in the kitchen cooking supper?"

"Yep, but I want you to get it."

… oh okay.
Sure.
Great.

I once heard that kids act the way they do around their mom because they feel **safe**.

And honestly, that tracks.

My husband will keep the kids for hours, and the second I walk in the door…

the whining starts,
the fussing begins,
the meltdowns activate.

He stands there stunned like,

"Y'all haven't done this all day! What happened?!"

Me.
*I* happened.

As moms, we're the nurturers.

We do things for our kids long after they actually need us to.

We still help with shoes.
We still cut their food —
(and I'll probably still be cutting grapes at their wedding).
We still fix their hair, pack their lunches, sign their papers,
kiss their boo-boos, remember their schedules, wash their uniforms,
and keep the whole operation running.

And because we do all that…

they come to us first.

Every.
Single.
Time.

But here's the *perspective shift* I'm working on:

Just because I CAN carry it doesn't mean I SHOULD carry it alone.

Sometimes I need to say:

"Look… they want me over here fixing hair.
Can you lessen the load by packing lunches?
Cleaning the kitchen?
Switching the laundry?
Doing literally anything that keeps me from combusting?"

Communication.

Still working on it.
Still learning.
Still trying not to snap when someone says,
"Did you need help?"
after I've been doing twenty things at once.

It's a process.

But the more I think about it…

the more I realize something beautiful:

They bypass Dad and come straight to me because I am their safe place.

I'm their comfort.
Their constant.
Their soft spot.
Their "Mom-watch-this!"
Their "Can-you-help-me?"
Their "I-need-you."

And even though it drains me…
and even though I get touched out…
and even though it sometimes makes me want to scream into a pillow…

one day they won't need me like this.

One day they will fix their own hair.
One day someone else will pack their lunch.
One day someone else will be the first person they call.

So I'm learning to see this season —
the bypassing Dad, going straight to Mom season —
as a **gift**.

Not always an easy one.

But a holy one.
A tender one.
A God-given one.

## Prayer

Jesus,
When my kids come to me first,
and I feel overwhelmed, tired,
or pulled in every direction,
help me see it as a gift — not a burden.

Remind me that being their safe place is sacred.
Give me patience when they bypass their dad
and strength to communicate the help I need.

Show me how to balance nurturing with boundaries,
and teach me to appreciate these moments
before they're gone.

**Amen.**

## REFLECTION QUESTIONS

*Take a moment to pause, breathe, and think about your day. Let these questions help you realize what mattered, what challenged you, and what blessed you.*

1. When do you feel the most overwhelmed by being the 'go-to' person, and why?

2. What support do you actually need–but haven't communicated yet?

# When the Mom Anxiety Gets Loud

Unfortunately, I've grown up with a nervous nature for as long as I can remember.

When I was young, I worried about getting sick, passing tests, forgetting homework — the everyday kid anxieties.

But as I got older, the worries grew up too.

Scarier things.
Bigger things.
The unknown.

My health.
My kids' health.

If I'm raising them right.
If I'm present enough.
If something could happen to me.

And then… there's Facebook.

Because nothing triggers an anxious mom faster than:

"It started with a headache and ended with stage 4 cancer."

Now I'm sitting there like:

Is my headache from my ponytail?
Or is it something worse?

Is this back pain because I slept wrong?
Or is it my kidney?

My brain goes from calm to panicking in 0.2 seconds.

And I hate that.

I hate how fear grabs onto a tiny thought and turns it into something huge.
I hate how fast my peace can disappear.
How loud my anxiety gets.
How easily the unknown overwhelms me.

But here's what I'm learning — slowly, breath by breath:

Anxiety is loud.
But **God is louder.**

If I stop long enough to listen.

Instead of letting fear fog my day, I'm trying to shift what voice I pay attention to.

And Jesus tells me clearly:

"So don't worry about tomorrow, for tomorrow will bring its own worries. Today's trouble is enough for today."
-Matthew 6:34 (NLT)

One day at a time.

Not tomorrow.
Not next year.
Not every terrifying "what if" my brain invents.

Just today.

And then He reminds me again:

"Look at the birds. They don't plant or harvest or store food in barns, for your heavenly Father feeds them. And aren't you far more valuable to Him than they are?"
-Matthew 6:26 (NLT)

Birds don't sit up at night spiraling.
Birds don't worry about outcomes.
Birds don't panic over every ache and twinge.

God takes care of them — and we are worth infinitely more to Him than birds.

If He feeds them, He will provide for us.
If He protects them, He will protect us.
If He watches over them, He is watching over us too.

And that truth changes things.
It gives me an entire new *perspective*.

Just take on today.

Not tomorrow.
Not the next twenty years.
Just this day.

God is faithful.
God is present.
God already knows tomorrow — so I don't have to.

And when the mom anxiety gets loud, I remind myself:

I am **never** facing the unknown alone.

## PRAYER

Jesus,
When my mind spirals and my fears get loud,
quiet my heart so I can hear Your voice
above every anxious thought.

Remind me that You care for the birds —
and You care for me even more.

Teach me to take life one day at a time,
trusting that You are already in tomorrow.

Give me peace when my body feels overwhelmed,
strength when my thoughts race,
and comfort when fear tries to take over.

Help me rest in the truth
that You hold my life, my health, my future,
and my children in Your hands.

**Amen.**

## REFLECTION QUESTIONS

*Take a moment to pause, breathe, and think about your day. Let these questions help you realize what mattered, what challenged you, and what blessed you.*

1. What worries tend to spiral the fastest for you, and what triggers them?

2. What would it look like to take life 'one day at a time' in a practical, real way?

# Apparently... I'm the One With the Attitude

Livie:
"Gosh Mom, why do you have an attitude?"
Me:
"Well, Livie… I didn't have an attitude the first four times I told you. How many times do I have to say it?"

Livie:
"Twelve…"

Somehow, after telling her to put her shoes on four times — FOUR — and she's still twirling around the living room like she has zero responsibilities in this world…

I'm the one with the attitude.

I can't make this up.

And honestly?
It's funny later.

But in the moment?

My eye is twitching,
my patience is fried,
and I feel like I'm talking to the wall.

And yet… somehow, some way…

I'm the one who ends up feeling bad afterward.

Because I snapped.
Because my tone changed.
Because I got frustrated.

Because moms carry guilt over EVERYTHING.

But today I tried to look at it differently.

What is another perspective?

Yes, I want her to listen.
Yes, I want her to hear me the first time.

But maybe there's another side to it…
a different perspective I'm trying to learn.

Maybe she's not ignoring me to be disrespectful.

Maybe she's just six.

Maybe she's in her own world —
happy and carefree, dancing around
because the day hasn't piled heavy on her shoulders yet.

And maybe —
*I'm the one who's distracted.*

I'm the one juggling a hundred things.
I'm the one whose brain is loud and full and tired.

And by the time she hears me...
I'm already at my limit.

So maybe this moment is less about:

"Why can't she listen?"

and more about:

"Lord, help **ME** slow down.
Help me speak with patience —
the first time,
to the fifth."

## PRAYER

Jesus,
Help me remember that she's little,
and sometimes I have to repeat myself —
just like You repeat Yourself to me.

Help me teach her gently and kindly,
before I react.

**Amen.**

## REFLECTION QUESTIONS

*Take a moment to pause, breathe, and think about your day. Let these questions help you realize what mattered, what challenged you, and what blessed you.*

1. When was the last time your frustration was more about your own stress than your child's behavior?

2. How might seeing the situation through your child's eyes change your response?

3. What would it look like to slow down your reaction in the next frustrating moment?

# No Secrets - Just Truth

Apparently nothing in my house is a secret anymore. I stopped at school and ran right into Emmie's teacher in the hallway.

Pre-K was a serious adjustment for my 4-year-old, and I'd been bribing her to stop crying with promises like:

"We'll go to the trampoline place."
"We'll go to Chuck E. Cheese."

Well… she told her teacher.

But that's not even the best part.

Emmie told her teacher she wanted to go to the park after school, but said:

"My mom might not want to… she might be busy."

Her teacher — bless her — said,

"Well, sometimes your mom has to do things around the house like clean and cook."

Emmie made the **BIGGEST** face and said:

"My mom? She don't cook."

Teacher:
"Your mama doesn't cook?"

Emmie:
"Nope. My daddy does. He makes rice & gravy, jambalaya, and crabs."

Teacher:
"Well what does your mama cook then?"

Emmie:
"Nothing."

**Rude.**
HILARIOUS.
But rude.

And at first, I was embarrassed.

Like… girl, you could've fibbed a LITTLE.

But when I thought about it later — once I stopped laughing at how she threw me straight under the bus — I realized something else— a different perspective.

She **notices**.

She sees who cooks.
She sees who cleans.
She sees who packs bags, answers emails, folds laundry,
fixes ponytails, finds lost shoes,
and holds everything together behind the scenes.

She doesn't always say it…
but she's paying attention.

And she'll realize later in life that it's us —
the mamas —
who are the glue to this family.

So maybe instead of feeling embarrassed…

maybe I should feel grateful that she's aware…
(even if she shares that information at the absolute worst possible time.)

## PRAYER

Jesus,
Thank You for stopping me in my tracks this morning
with that reminder:
"The enemy forgets that a shadow is proof of light."

Help me remember that even in the messy moments,
the uncomfortable ones,
the "why did she say THAT?" moments…
there is still light shining somewhere.

Even in the parts of motherhood
that feel exposing or embarrassing,
You are there — in the truth, in the connection,
in the tiny hints of grace woven through it all.

Help me laugh more, breathe deeper,
and not take myself so seriously
when my kids tell the world my business.

Help me see the purpose behind their honesty,
and trust that Your light is shining over us.

**Amen.**

## REFLECTION QUESTIONS

*Take a moment to pause, breathe, and think about your day. Let these questions help you realize what mattered, what challenged you, and what blessed you.*

1. What parts of motherhood make you feel most exposed or judged?

2. Where can you find humor or light in moments that feel embarrassing or uncomfortable?

# Press Your Heart

Since school started, we've had this little morning ritual — drawing *tiny* hearts on each other's hands before drop-off.

Nothing fancy.
Just a pen.
Just a heart.

But it's become one of my favorite parts of the day.

Most mornings it's sweet…
and some mornings it's chaos.

We'll be rolling into the school line and suddenly:

"WAIT!! We forgot our hearts!"

Cue the scrambling.

"Mama, unbuckle me! I need to draw Sissy's heart right now!"

So there I am —
stretching across the seats,
dodging book bags,
drawing a crooked heart
while the car line inches forward.

It's messy.
It's rushed.
It's **us**.

When they're at school, I tell them,

"If you press your heart, I'll feel it."

Every day Emmie asks,

"Mama… did you feel me press my heart today?"

And I always say yes.

Because I do —
not physically,
but deep in my chest,
every time I think of them.

Kids don't know how often we think of them.

How much of our day revolves around them.
How even our date nights get planned around them.

But this is where Jesus meets me —

in the love that's almost too big for my chest.
in the constant thoughts.
in the way I'd choose them every time.

If my love for them is this strong...
let me think of it in a *different* perspective.

How much stronger must His love be for me?

One day they won't be asking me to redraw a heart in the car line.
One day they won't press a little marker heart at school and wonder if I felt it.

These simple, chaotic, sweet moments?

They won't last forever.

And if these small things mean so much to me...

how much more must God cherish the small ways I reach for Him?

## PRAYER

Jesus,
Thank You for meeting me in the little moments —
in the hearts on our hands,
in the quick hugs before school,
and in the tiny rituals that remind us we're connected.

Help me slow down enough
to see the sweetness in the rush
and feel Your love the same way my children feel mine.

Thank You for every season,
every moment,
and every reminder of the love we share.

**Amen.**

## **REFLECTION QUESTIONS**

*Take a moment to pause, breathe, and think about your day. Let these questions help you realize what mattered, what challenged you, and what blessed you.*

1. What small daily routines remind you of the love between you and your children?

2. What 'little moments' have meant more to you than you realized at the time?

# Shoes or No Shoes

THANK GOD — literally — that about halfway to church I noticed BOTH of my children did NOT grab their shoes from the door like I told them to.

Too busy breathing in each other's direction, apparently.

Me:
"Livie, put your shoes on."

Livie:
long dramatic groan
"uhhh…"

Me:
"You're kidding right? Emmie??"

Emmie:

"me eida…"
(Translation: "me either" in toddler language)

So there I was…

In my church clothes…
Trying to get my spirit right…

And then quickly pulling into a Dollar Store like a NASCAR driver.

And honestly, it would've been SO easy to just turn around and go home.

We were already running late.
I could've said, "Forget it, we tried," and called it a day.

But something in me pushed forward.

And that's when it hit me — *a different perspective:*

God will always get us where we're going — shoes or no shoes.

Shoes or no shoes, it's important that we keep moving **forward**.

There will always be something trying to slow us down or knock us off our path.

But our goal — as mamas, as women, as people —

is to be a little bit further than we were yesterday.
Further than we were last month.
Further than we were last year.

Forward is forward.

Even if it's messy.
Even if it's chaotic.
Even if you had to buy Dollar Store shoes on the way to church.

Progress is still progress.

Sometimes motherhood feels like a series of interruptions and inconveniences.

But maybe… just maybe…

these tiny chaotic moments are actually small reminders of God's faithfulness.

Little lessons dressed up as chaos.

Proof that even when we're scrambling, He's still making a way.

He still gets us there.
Right on time.
Every time.

**Shoes or no shoes.**

## PRAYER

Jesus,
Please don't let the little things discourage us.
Remind us that things rarely go as planned,
and that's okay.

When the path shifts,
help us trust that You're still making a way.

Help us remember that a detour isn't a disaster —
it's often Your protection,
Your timing,
Your gentle redirection.

And Lord…
Thank You for being the God
who would rather see us walk in five minutes late
than not come at all.

Help me show up, try again, keep going,
and trust that You will always get us
where we're meant to be —
shoes or no shoes.
**Amen.**

## REFLECTION QUESTIONS

*Take a moment to pause, breathe, and think about your day. Let these questions help you realize what mattered, what challenged you, and what blessed you.*

1. Where in your life do you need to give yourself permission to keep going, even if it's messy?

2. What recent 'detour' might have been protection or redirection rather than failure?

# Teaching Tiny Hearts

Parenting will humble you fast.

    A few weeks ago, we had one of those days —
the kind that should've been simple,
but somehow turned into a lesson
I didn't even realize we needed.

We spent the morning out in town:

breakfast at Mr. Ronnie's Donut Shop,
ran a few errands,
grabbed some lunch,

and then — of course —

we ended up at Target.

Somewhere between the women's section and the toy aisles,
both kids were begging for everything in sight.

And the second I finally stopped to look at something for myself, I
heard:

"Moooom, we've been here an hour!"

Meanwhile I'm thinking,

Do y'all even realize how lucky you are?

But they're six and four.
They don't see it yet.

So we tried showing them that if they wanted things,
they had to earn money for the purchases they wanted —

because things don't just appear.
They come from work.
From sacrifice.
From money.

But, naturally…
that didn't stick forever.

However, everything came full circle when it was time for our yearly
Samaritan's Purse Christmas boxes.

We were standing in the toy section again —

this time choosing gifts for a little boy and a little girl somewhere across the world.

Children who don't walk into Target.
Children who don't beg for ten things they don't need.
Children who don't get to live in the kind of abundance mine don't even realize is abundance.

My girls were fussing and crying about the toys they weren't getting, and there I was holding a tiny toothbrush and a simple hairbrush, explaining:

"These are privileges to some kids.
This little box might be the only gift they get this year."

They looked back at me, confused and frustrated —
and I had to remind myself:

Of course they don't understand.
They're not supposed to.

But it's my job to keep teaching them —
seed by seed,
moment by moment,
until one day it finally clicks.

Because perspective doesn't land all at once.

It grows quietly,
through ordinary days
and inconvenient lessons.

One day they'll understand the blessing it is just to:

wake up healthy...
stand on their own feet...
open their eyes...
brush their teeth...
go to school...
drink clean water...
sleep in a safe home...

and yes —

to go to Disney World.

Blessings big and small,
woven into the everyday.

## PRAYER

Jesus,
give our children eyes to see the blessings around them —
the loud ones,
the quiet ones,
the small ones,
the big ones,
and the ones tucked into ordinary moments.

Give them grateful hearts,
gentle spirits,
and true perspective.

And give us, as their parents,
the wisdom and patience
to guide them into understanding.

Help us teach gratitude
not through perfection,
but through consistent reminders
of Your goodness.

**Amen.**

## REFLECTION QUESTIONS

*Take a moment to pause, breathe, and think about your day. Let these questions help you realize what mattered, what challenged you, and what blessed you.*

1. What "seed moments" can I be more intentional about planting, even if they don't understand yet?

2. How often do I model gratitude in front of my children—not just talk about it?

3. What everyday blessings have I started seeing as "normal" instead of "abundant"?

# Letter to The Mamas

Hey sister,
I hope you see that motherhood — all of it —
is the most chaotic, exhausting, beautiful,
rewarding experience we'll ever walk through.

I searched high and low for a book I could relate to…
something real, something honest,
something that didn't make me feel like I was failing
because my life didn't feel perfect.

And as I was searching,
I was also digging into my faith more deeply.

I kept praying the same simple prayer:

"Jesus, show me You hear me.
Use me if You will.
Help my mindset.
Guide me.
Teach me to be more patient…
please teach me to be more understanding with my children."

Because honestly?

I felt constantly overwhelmed.
Overstimulated.

Like I was drowning in noise, mess, schedules, emotions…
all of it.

And then — when I least expected it —
He literally woke me up at 2 a.m. out of a dead sleep.
(FYI, Jesus… 8 a.m. would've been alright too.)

But that night?

**I wrote this book.**

And I have never heard Him more clearly.

Words flowed out of me like never before.
I didn't even realize what was happening
until I got up the next morning,
not remembering half of what I wrote.

I just sat there and thought,

Oh my… I think God *spoke* to me.

I didn't hear Him audibly —
but He was in my mind, guiding every word.

This is my testimony.
I have a testimony.

If even one person reads these pages and says,

"Wow… I'm not alone,"

then I've done what He asked me to do.

Because if ANYTHING, sister…

I hope you take away the same truth I learned while writing this:

It's all about **perspective**.

I *shifted* mine —
and it changed **everything**.

Motherhood didn't get easier.
Life didn't suddenly calm down.
My kids didn't magically stop being wild.

But my heart softened.
My guilt loosened.
My patience stretched.
My faith deepened.

I stopped seeing myself as a "bad mom"
and started seeing myself as a good mama —
one who is still learning, still growing, still showing up…
even when I'm tired, messy, or imperfect.

And so are **you**.

You're not alone.
You're not failing.
You're not behind.

You're a mama doing her best in a world
that demands too much of us
and gives too little grace in return.

So here's my prayer for you:

May your perspective shift.
May your heart breathe again.
May you see the beauty tucked inside the chaos.
May you remember that Jesus is in the middle of all of it —
every tantrum, every tear, every late morning, every blessing.

And may you always know…

You are a **good** mama.
Better than you think.
Stronger than you feel.
And absolutely never alone.

# Letter to My Mama

ama,

    You set the bar way too high.

So many times you show up to my house
ready to help — just hands on deck.

To tackle my house,
my laundry,
my girls,

or simply to sit with me
and talk.

A SHIFT IN PERSPECTIVE

You made me
and shaped me
into who I am today.

You always put me first.
You never missed a game or an event.

You made me confident in myself,
taught me to always try my best…

and only ever let me quit swim team
that one time when I was five.

You are my best friend.
My ride or die.
The queen.
Shuggie.

And my favorite title of all —

**my Mama**.

Thank you.

For everything you've done,
everything you still do,
and everything you never let me see you struggle through.

I love you *more*.

What a blessing you have been —
and still are —
to me.

KAITLIN FOLSE LEBEOUF

I cherish you
and our relationship
more than you know.

I pray I can be even half the mama
you've been to me.

If I manage that,
my girls will be blessed
beyond measure.

# Letter to My Girls

My sweet baby girls,
I love you both so much
it makes my heart ache.

Sometimes I look at you
and wish I could scoop you up
and keep you little forever —

the tiny voices,
the ringlets,
the personality,
all of it.

But at the same time,
I can't wait to see who you become.

I'm always preparing you for the next stage,
cheering you into the next milestone...

and then when it gets here,
I'm like,

"Wait... I wasn't ready for that."

You're growing so fast.

Your daddy and I
are so proud of you both.

Keep being the light that you are.
Be kind.
And always, always follow Jesus.

I promise to lift you up,
support you,
love you,
correct you,
and laugh with you.

I promise to show up —
even when I'm tired,
even when I feel like I'm failing,
even when motherhood feels heavy.

You both make the heavy parts
worth carrying.

But I also want to thank you.

Thank you for teaching me.
Thank you for guiding me.
Thank you for shaping me
into the woman and mother I am today.

Thank you for giving me grace —
even when you don't realize you're giving it —

because I'm just a mama
figuring it all out too.

I will always do my best.
And I will always love you,
more than life itself.

      \* \* \*

And to my babies in Heaven —

one day, when I get there,
I know I'll hear

"Hey Mama"

from two little voices
I've never heard here on earth…

and I'll love you
just the same.

# Daily Perspective Prayers

"Jesus, meet me where I am… and shift my perspective so I can see You in all of this."

"Lord, shift my perspective — remind me I'm not a bad mom, I'm just a full-on mom, a growing mom, a trying mom."

"God, shift my perspective so I can see my children through Your eyes — with patience and compassion."

"Jesus, shift my perspective today. Help me see what You're showing me, not just what's in front of me."

"Jesus, shift my perspective when frustration rises. Quiet my spirit and calm my reactions."

"Lord, shift my perspective and help me keep stepping forward — shoes or no shoes — trusting that progress is still progress."

"God, shift my perspective and remind me I am doing better than I think I am."

"Jesus, shift my perspective so I pause before I snap and breathe before I break."

"Lord, shift my perspective to see the blessings — the loud ones, the quiet ones, the small ones, and the ones tucked into ordinary moments."

"Jesus, shift my perspective and help me release guilt and receive grace when I need rest."

"Lord, shift my perspective and remind me my children don't need perfection — they need presence."

"God, shift my perspective when I feel overwhelmed; steady me, strengthen me, and center me again."

"Jesus, shift my perspective — I am not failing; I am learning and growing too."

"Lord, shift my perspective to celebrate the small, crooked, messy moments that matter most."

"God, shift my perspective so I see motherhood differently — with gratitude, softness, and grace for myself."

# Closing

If you take anything from this book,
I hope it's this:

You don't have to change your whole life
to feel lighter…

you just have to **shift**
how you see it.

Motherhood won't suddenly get quiet.
Kids won't magically stop needing you.
Chaos won't disappear.

But your perspective
can change everything.

A SHIFT IN PERSPECTIVE

And if there's one prayer
I want you to carry from these pages,
it's this:

**"Jesus, meet me where I am…
and shift my perspective
so I can see You in all of this."**

Because once you start noticing
the blessings tucked inside
your everyday moments—

the crooked hearts in the car line,
the shoes that never seem to be
on the right feet,
the loud mornings that somehow
become sweet memories—

you'll realize you weren't failing.

You were growing.

One *shift* in *perspective*
at a time.

# Acknowledgments

To my girls —
thank you for being the best,
hardest,
funniest part of my life.

You made me a mama,
and that changed everything.

To my husband —
thank you for believing in the woman
I would grow to become
back when we were just sixteen.

Thank you for supporting me,
for making fun of me just to make me laugh,
for pushing me,
for never doubting me,

and of course…
for cooking us the best meals
and keeping our bellies full.

KAITLIN FOLSE LEBEOUF

I love you more than you know.

To my mama —
thank you for showing up for me
in ways I didn't even know I needed.

I am who I am because of you.
I hope this book makes you proud.

To my friends —
the ones who listen to me fuss,
complain,
cry,
laugh,
and spiral...
but never judge.

I love you,
and I truly couldn't do motherhood —
or life —
without your listening ears
and open hearts.

And to Jesus —
thank You for choosing me,
waking me up at 2 a.m.,
shifting my perspective,
and handing me every word on these pages.

This book is my testimony...
and all glory goes to You.

## About the Author

Kaitlin Folse Lebeouf is a wife to her high school sweetheart, a mama to two daughters, and a woman learning to find Jesus in the chaos of everyday motherhood. She writes the way she lives — honest, imperfect, and always searching for the blessings tucked inside ordinary moments. When she's not juggling school drop-offs and travel-agent clients, she's traveling with her family and learning to savor the season she's in — stretched thin, but giving it everything she has. Her hope is simple: that every mama who opens this book feels seen, understood, and a little less alone.

www.ingramcontent.com/pod-product-compliance
Lightning Source LLC
Chambersburg PA
CBHW050522100526
44581CB00002B/72